Edited by Shaun Russell

FIRST EDITION
- 2023 -

ISBN: 978-1-915439-87-1

Published by
Candy Jar Books
Mackintosh House
136 Newport Road, Cardiff, CF24 1DJ
www.candyjarbooks.co.uk

Printed and bound in the UK by
Severn, Bristol Road, Gloucester, GL2 5EU

Jean and the Queen

MATT LEWIS

Illustrated by Tom Burchell

If you listen in the garden,
Somewhere up in the trees,
You'll hear a humming, buzzing noise.
It's coming from the bees.

They live inside a hive,
In each one there is a queen,
But in this hive's a special bee,
And this bee's name is Jean.

Jean, she is a little bee,
With wings that aren't quite straight.
So when she leaves the hive for work,
She's almost always late!

She zig-zags around the orchard.
She spirals through the flowers.
She sometimes crashes into things.
She's buzzing around for hours.

Jean wants to be a pollinator,
Like all the other bees.
But instead of landing on the flowers,
She's bumping into trees.

The other bees are busy,
And soon fall out with Jean.
"If you carry on like this
We'll report you to the queen!"

She can’t land on as many plants
As the others do each day.
As she flies, she flips and dives,
Getting in the workers’ way.

So instead she goes exploring,
Each time a different route,
Past vegetable beds and flower heads,
Through trees full up with fruit.

Then as the sun goes down each night,
The bees they all head back,
To drop off all of the pollen
That they've collected in a stack.

But today was very different
When little Jean arrived.
The bees were waiting for her
As she buzzed into the hive.

"We've told the queen, you lazy bee,
You never do your work."
"You just wait, she's on her way,"
They hummed, and buzzed, and smirked.

And just then, the queen arrived,
Surrounded by her guards.
“Move out of the way! Now let me see,
This bee that won’t work hard!”

Jean took a gulp and fumbled forward.
She'd never met the queen,
Who's always there but hidden away,
And very rarely seen.

When Jean appeared, the queen let out
An almighty roaring laugh!
"Is this the bee I need to see?"
The others agreed, then gasped.

"Oh, silly bees!" she said with anger!
"It's you who are in trouble.
Just look at Jean and you will see,
She's in a massive pollen bubble."

It turns out that when poor Jean
Had bumped, and spun, and flew,
She had collected lots more pollen
Than any other bee could do!

The bees they were amazed!
They cheered for little Jean,
As she's now the greatest pollinator
That the hive has ever seen!

To my son, Freddie.
BEE amazing, BEE kind,
but most of all BEE yourself.